Finding Our Way Back to Eden

Zo Owen, M.A.

iUniverse, Inc.
New York   Bloomington

Finding Our Way Back to Eden

iUniverse books may be ordered through booksellers or by contacting:

iUniverse
1663 Liberty Drive
Bloomington, IN 47403
www.iuniverse.com
1-800-Authors (1-800-288-4677)

Because of the dynamic nature of the Internet, any Web addresses or links contained in this book may have changed since publication and may no longer be valid.

For information on cover art work contact Kathy Muro @ bythesee@optonline.net

Contact Zo Owen at: yourspiritcounselor@yahoo.com

ISBN: 978-1-4401-3174-5 (pbk)
ISBN: 978-1-4401-3175-2 (ebk)

Library of Congress Control Number: 2009925666

Printed in the United States of America

iUniverse rev. date: 4/7/2009

This work is dedicated to my parents,
who now live in Spirit,
with my love and appreciation.
All I know of kindness,
I learned from these two remarkable
people.

Their absence is present, their presence,
felt.

ACKNOWLEDGMENTS

I would like to thank everyone who helped me bring this book forward and to bow in the direction of the true and faithful, unseen forces, that informed me and filled me with a courage far beyond my personality ranges.

Thank you to my beloved and respected Teacher, W. Brugh Joy, M.D. an extraordinary Teacher of Consciousness, whose personal exploration of the mysteries of healing and the multiplicity of selves, is best expressed through his own works, "Joy's Way" and "Avalanche". I recommend visiting his web site, www.brughjoy.com, for more information.

Thank you to Kathy Taylor Muro for the cover design. Her ability to capture the essence of what I wanted to express and bring through the marvelous image on the cover, is appreciated.

Thank you to Amy E. Taylor for editorial assistance and for her marvelous wit, that made our work together a joy.

To Mark Taylor and Jon Muro, for providing tech support.

To Jim, for his confidence in me.

Finally thank you to my many friends and colleagues who expressed appreciation for my writing.

Namaste

Foreword

What a fool I am. This is the least yet most potent attack among the barrage of depth doubts inhibiting my pen as I approach writing this foreword. Foolish, to be sure, as I know very little about the intellectual appreciation of poetry, its styles, classes, exoteric and esoteric mysteries. Another wave of anxiety sweeps through me as I begin to consider guiding readers into the profundity of Eden.

Suddenly a salvational realization erupts into my awareness. Perhaps it is a fool's experience of life that most approximates Eden…a fool's paradise precluded to the very intelligent. In that case…and certainly in regards to my relationship to poetry I DO qualify. I stumble and ramble from one poet to another, from one poem to another, from word to word yet I seem to experience Grace, by heaven only knows what, that stirs words into no words buoyed by an association anthology of feelings. Is this one of the Edens into which Zo Owen's poetry "Finding Our Way Back To Eden" births me? Is Forest Gump's foolish life just one paradisiacal poem after another…each episode delivering him into Eden after Eden physically, psychologically, and spiritually? Does my anxious educated and socially conditioned thinking occult my own manifested Edens?

The poems in this splendid gathering rest in the shade of The Eden Tree of Transcendent Consciousness. Zo's poetry compels a fracture in the traditional understanding of Paradise. She sometimes confronts, cajoles, seduces, tantalizes, sets apart, and flashes fire burning away illusions and delusions to offer our much needed blackened still blinking eyes the trailhead governed by the Call to "Finding Our Way Back to Eden".

W. Brugh Joy, M. D.

Introduction

When I began to consider presenting a collection of my poems, I had my own ideas on the form it would take however, the form it took, was a form generated by deeper forces. I could say that about my life and it would be equally accurate.

The title for this collection dropped itself into my awareness and began as a series of reflections and meditations on Eden, Paradise and The Fall. Each of these, worthy of separate deliberation and expression, percolated into a final form.

What seems most true for me, is that Eden is not a place, nor has it ever been a place, but rather a metaphor for an inner experience of a paradisaical state of unity. It is the home we miss and long for and yet, it is the home we have never really left, nor has "It" ever, left us.

I believe returning to the inner Eden, is an experience the soul intends for each of us to have. The soul is eternally patient.

I am inclined to believe that the best poetry, whatever it's intentions, is a kind of theology, while theology generally is bad poetry.

--Harold Bloom

Contents

Eden

One day,
she found
what she had never known
she had lost.

Certainly there were always whispers of "more than this",
but whispers are not demands,
these would come later.

Slowly it rose from inside her
the reconciliation,
the befriending of opposites,
the memory of Eden,
the paradise of inner union,
the palpable love for her own sweet animal body
and the music that came from it.

She found, what she had sought,
had been seeking her,
as a lover seeks the beloved.

This was the paradise promised,
to love one's own being

Paradise, the fall and the return.

Original Sin

There never was an Original Sin...
Birth with the condition of redemption
is an unholy value.

Redemption was never sought,
until the spontaneity of
the natural world, frightened
dark minds and small hearts.

Original Grace is the antidote
for this poison.
The truth of Grace, as our
intended state, is one,
the Christ, would embrace.

The world will not be transformed
by more sacrifice, enough blood
is on the altars of the world.

If transformation comes it will
be through the outpouring of Grace
and we have never needed it more.

A Tendency Towards Complexity

and what if...
I am,
as the Universe is,
as God is,
always in cycles of motion,
recognized or unrecognized,
welcomed or shunned,
yet
always
moving
towards
a complexity of diversity
and its physical expression.

No longer a single face
thats true or truth
but a collage of faces and truths

Would not I and God, become more inclusive,
tolerant and loving, dark and destructive,
finally becoming the one beautiful and
terrifying face of Consciousness.

Rolling Along

You can't tell a ball rolling down hill,
to notice. it is a ball, rolling down hill...
since it is, both the ball,
and the hill.

A Dream Within A Dream

I dreamt, I dreamt
and in the dreaming
found myself
embraced by
childhood friends
and
lovers of another time.

Maybe this, is the greatest truth
if truth can be stated to be true at all,
we all come to play our parts in life

and perhaps,
even the people I never cared for much,
loved me sufficiently within their soul
to be part of my play

and perhaps,
I loved them
quite beyond a conscious personal preference,
loved sufficiently
to serve them in return.

A dream is a dream...

and the dreamer
swims in seas quite beyond
what the personality can
imagine.

Awakening

When first we broke
with the darkness
of unknowing
and set our feet
on the path towards the light,
something shuddered,
reluctantly releasing its children
to take small, tentative steps
towards Self-realization

The Dark Night

It is no small thing,
nor a wonder,
that each of us, wounded,
wounds.

True,
some forgive with immediacy
and bless them, but in a truth,
of a another consideration,
we each may need, periods of relief
from the brilliance of the sun.

Perhaps, this is why, night
with her deep understanding
of human nature,
covers us for a time
with a compassionate darkness.

And Then

When I awoke,
I knew, I did not know.
Humility was the gift in the not knowing.

I looked for sages, so I might know,
as knowing seemed more powerful.

then,
I began to think I knew, at least sometimes.

Humility became muted and a delicious sense of
certainty began to rise.

I became intoxication with the illusion of power,
and with that, came spiritual arrogance.

then,
one day, a small, quiet day,
I recognized, knowing was far less prized by my soul,
than loving.

I imagine I will circle round a few more times before
I am sure, of what I am sure of ...

I don't know ...

Small Things

And I wondered that morning,
that brilliantly sunny morning
I found a lady bug on a leaf of a flower near my door,
if I had displaced my attention on to no-sense things
and forgotten
the wonder of the small.

The world can be so horrific and
we humans, so bestial as to give the beasts themselves, pause,
sending an impulse of appreciation into the world,
is more an imperative than a romantic gesture.

Perhaps, in the end, it will be the small things,
that save us or destroy us?

Opening

She had everything she always
felt would bring happiness,
a partner, children, a home
by the sea, and still
happiness eluded her.
She saw it in the faces of others,
she tasted it on her tongue,
her heart, hurt a little all the time,
hungering for "some thing".

It was in that moment
in the darkest of nights
when everything she knew failed her,
the moment she cried out
to her God, she could finally hear
her soul deliver the question
that would change her life forever.

"What about me?"

Light As A Metaphor

Good poems fraction off the individual experience,
like light hitting the prisms of a a crystal,
each color reclaiming its unique identity.

Ah, but great poetry is Transpersonal.
It concentrates our essence
like light through a magnifying lens,
focusing
into a single, burning remembering,
the memory of unity
at the core of the experience of being.

Your Father

I want to tell my children about their father,
tell them something of who this man was,
tell them, something fine, about him.

I never recognized what mirrors we were
to each other's insecurities,
how we unconsciously collaborated to support
each other's facades,
how we gave over to each other
the parts of ourselves
we didn't want to carry,
like giving over baggage at an airport or hotel
only this baggage was stuff we had packed long
before the marriage and dragged around with us.

I want to tell them their father liked to fish
and that he could make a really decent breakfast,
that he was a very competent person in the world,
though at times, he cared a bit too much
that others knew it.
He was funny, hard as it is now to believe that.
He made me laugh. I felt safe with him.

Looking at him today those things don't seem present
and its possible they never were,
that love and projection created the Ed that I saw,
but then none of us escape the building of a persona
only to carve away at it later in life to find
for ourselves, what is authentically us and what is
clothing we've put over it.

I know for sure, he did love you
and loves you still, despite
the appearance of pettiness and petulance.

He is a man who has lost his way
and fears finding it.
I don't know if that is of any comfort,
sometimes anger feels better than sorrow,
but you come from something fine, and
I want you to know that.

Whale Watcher

We were looking for whales that day
following the migratory route
of the wonderful grey humpbacks
up from the Baja to the Monterey Peninsula,
a migratory route encoded into their being.

The boat rode very low in the high black swells
and the sight of our land horizon
fell and returned again.

We rode in quiet for a long while
with only the hum of the motor and
the screech and cry of the sea birds above us.

Suddenly I felt the sea was breathing
and I, was breathing with her.
Her inhalations drawing me down into her dark bosom
and her exhalations and my own, lifting me
again up into the spray and the sunlight.

Death and resurrection.
Death and resurrection.
Death and resurrection.

Durga

She had swum in a sea of aborted possibilities
for so long, happiness seemed an absurd expectation.

Finding Love At A Funeral

We met again at the funeral
of a mutual friend
decades after we had parted
with fingers pointing at each other.

Its funny how funerals will bring you
nose to nose with your own life
and how you've lived it,
especially if there is more of it
behind you, than in front.

It startled me to see him there,
the dark curly hair, grey now,
his face fuller.

Somewhere over the coffee and cake,
we tentatively found each other
and love rushed back in.

I tried to remember all the bad moments,
the unfulfilled expectations,
the first falling away of all positive projections,
but all I could touch was loving appreciation
and joy, in knowing he still existed, somewhere.

Where, was immaterial to me.

I introduced my husband, he introduced his wife
and I knew we were both exactly
where each of us needed to be.

Nothing had been a mistake,

we had not been a mistake.
We each had been bridges
to the loves, we had now.

We embraced when I left like two old war buddies.
He said, "I will always remember you as that smart,
skinny blonde girl who always wore a pony tail.
That's never going to change."

I smiled and said,
"Thanks, I am counting on that."

Laughing Buddha

This morning, I wonder
if its not we
who insist consciousness
can only come through
trial and suffering.

I wonder if the Deity
is not totally bored by now
with how determined
we seem to be, to resist joy
as a Spiritual path?

Perhaps joy has come to appear
a little less Sacred
and suffering has taken
its crown of thorns
and wears it as a
trophy, mocking joy
as trivial and unworthy?

Hate – The Cast Out Goddess

I want to speak for Hate now,
the cast out Goddess, with her dark,
delicious infusion of indifference
and her venomous tongue.
Costumed as spider, worshiped
as Balaat, she is the voice of
liberated darkness
and she stands without apology,
in direct opposition to the sun.

The Long Way Round

She took the longest way round to say
what she wanted to express.
It required a good deal
of patience and
compassion
to sit
and
listen
for
it.

She wrote
the same way,
writing a labyrinth of material
before finding her center, before finding
what it was, that could be excavated from the
battery of abstractions she lived with as daily thought.

The Janus Coin

And what if, there are Gods who find Love, an anathema,
and Grace, pathetic,

Gods who wish to walk naked and arrogant, in places Sacred
to the pious.

Gods who have no interest in philosophical discourse or
theological principle,

Deities who yawn, when showered with language of Transformation
and Evolution.

Best give them some room, some space on your altar,
lest they drag us into their powerful mischief.

To Be Still, For Another

There is a time,
a time when less is more,
and good enough,
is good enough.

A time when what we say,
is held within a bit longer,
and so, heard more deeply
by the one speaking.

At this time,
with grace perhaps,
and the prayers
of those who love us,
our need to be heard,
is less urgent
than our interest in listening.

To be still,
for another,
is a Sacred act.

Closure

I think it takes more to close
with kindness, when closing is asked for,
than to open, when invited.

Holding there is no heroine
no hero, and no one outside
the dance, is a staggering piece
of consciousness.

It was so delicious, to blame.
I kind of hate to surrender it,
but I have experienced the consequences
of blaming.

I want to, want to,
gracefully surrender when timing
directs a closure and do it
with a blessing.

I want to, want to,
release irritating people,
unforgiven hurts,
expectations,
and current disappointments.

I want to, want to,
and
it is, I feel
a beginning.

Musing

If I can only hold that everything and
everyone in my life is just as they are
and doing what they do, without
holding a judgment or preference

If I can hold my very personal life, impersonally,
but still tenderly and with enormous appreciation.

I shall be doing very, very well, I think.

Lazarus

He had a small purse of a mouth with narrow,
tight lips, that spoke a poverty of expression.

His determination to defend against loss, kept
him from opening his mouth and singing.

The Church As Eve Intended

She was a church but not in the image
of the church today.

No, she was a rowdy church,
that knew her share of suffering and
loved her pint or two, sitting on her
front porch in the evening.

One that loved the kind of rascal
who could sing a good tune and
tell stories that would make you laugh
till your eyes teared.

Rascals who could play the small accordion,
while everyone stomped on the floor
to its rhythm and one that kept her money
in in old tea tin in the cupboard.

She loved her family more than she loved her God
and in my heart, I think even God dare not
challenge her on this.

We the woman of her clan, women of music,
song and story, are the church and we are
not the breast beating ones whose brilliant red
hair are covered with black scarfs to keep the
devil away....No, we invite the devil to dance
with us, after all, is he not also God?

Though my own soul lines up more
with my father's quiet nature,
there is at my center, the dark Eros
the Irish have always carried.

The men who love us are warriors
and somehow we find in each other,
the Divine, Itself.

Requiem

She said she was dying
and I believe she was.

She said it was from an illness
but I felt it was a refusal
to surrender her outrage.

I asked if she really wanted to live
and she said not if it meant forgiving.

The Child With The Radiant Heat

There once was a child with a radiant heart.

Everyone who stood near the child could feel her heart's warmth.

Anyone who was feeling alone or frightened
could see it's bright light.

And their own heart's, grew and grew, until
they too, had radiant hearts,
that looked liked sunshine
coming through a clear window.

The child became a grown up and her heart
touched everyone with her kindness.

The young woman became a mother,
then a grandmother and finally,
an old person, still
her heart shone brightly, as if
it were brand new.

One day the old person left to go back
to the God that had created her.

Everyone missed her, so they talked
of how good they felt
when they thought of her.

They said she made you feel
like the best thing since apple pie.

And their own hearts grew warm

and filled with a light
that felt very much like
she was present among them
once again.

Anger

I opened the closet door that morning
and found Anger was there.
It sat on the counter next to the
place I make my morning coffee
and lay next to my toothbrush.

I said to Anger, "Why are you here?"
and she answered, "Haven't you noticed
I live here. I've lived here for a long while now."

Falling Backward Into The Abyss

Falling backward into the abyss
I loose myself,
surrendering to the fall
surrendering to the descent
into that dark place,
the womb of the world,
and there, I am caught
by the outstretched arms
of the Mother of All Beginnings,
only to discover the dark mother
from whom I have fled all these years,
is She, who loves me most.

Empty

There is something hungry
in the face of my friend,
something starved.

The too thin face, the body,
aerobicized into leanness
with no body fat left
to mediate for softness.

What is it this face wants?

Can it be purchased in a health food store
or Chinese apothecary, rubbed into the skin
carried on sesame oil, found by breathing
deeper and more slowly with the latest,
best yoga teacher in L.A.?

This morning I'm thinking that face
is reflecting the soul's hunger to know love
of the kind and quality it came from....
and all the rest, is tap dancing.

The Brown Cowl

He has the seductively innocent hands of a young priest,
long, phallic fingers, unlined white skin
drawn tightly over bone.
In his body movement, lifetimes of discipline,
bare feet in brown sandals
stepping softly over monastery floors
of smooth grey stone.

Carrying the Great Silence.

Crocus

I know there is a God in nature
by the way crocus push up through
the snow, towards the light.

It is a simple statement of Faith.

Untitled

In poetry we stand naked,
making our most personal experiences
palpable to strangers.

Goddess of Discord Having a Really Bad Day

It seems there are times
when shit just runs down hill
with amazing velocity
and there is no getting out of the way.

I am willing to consider my share of the karmic implications,
but I prefer the idea that there is
a Goddess of Discord on a mountain top somewhere
and collectively, we have really pissed her off,
to the counter proposition of random acts of violence.

At least the former, has a bit of soul.

Inspiration

Inspiration does not wait for the laundry to be folded.
It does not allow you to fall back to sleep at three o'clock in the
morning,
when a wonderful first line repeats itself, over and over in your mind,
growing fuller with each repetition.

I have learned to surrender to writing.

I write on everything, bank deposit slips, grocery receipts,
odd pieces of scrap paper, phrases written everywhere,
looking for consolidation and expression.

Writing poetry is like tending a child.
It has an immediacy that must be respected.

The Cocktail Party

The shame of it, lay
not in his withholding from her,
small kindnesses and courtesies,
nor in his thinly veiled attacks on
her opinions in the company of others,
no, anger, would have at least been honest.

The shame lay in his not being courageous
enough to own, he envied her ability to feel.

Faith

Today the wind is fierce,
It whips the surf and
bends the trees into submission.
I watch the gulls overhead
glide sideways within this force,
as they allow wind and Spirit
to dictate their direction,
without complaint.

Knowing And Not Knowing

Who knows?
God knows.
God is everywhere.
That use to confuse me when I was a child,
it made me uneasy to think God could see me in the bathroom.

Is God true or metaphorical?
What is truth anyway?
Is truth ever really possible?
Are there Divine truths?

Have you ever argued with someone
insisting your truth, was the truth?
....and how the hell would we know anyway,
truth being the slippery thing it is.

Did you ever try to speak your truth as a child,
nervously shifting your weight from one foot to the other,
uncomfortable in your own body?

Yes....body language is an interesting thing,
the hand across the solar plexus,
a little boy's hand protecting his penis.

Suppose ...WE are the only language God has?

Lucifer, The Light Bearer

How can we condemn a being who so loved his creator
he could not bend his knee to those made from clay,
or was it hubris, that kept him in rebellion to the
service asked of him?

Was it really a sacrifice, this apparent fall from grace,
was it essential we have the duality of good and evil
for this plane so the Deity could know itself?

Who is to say, why one soul will take on the incarnatory cloak
of darkest evil and another clothe their essence in white?

Who is to say, how the horrors in service to evil
can serve the collective, when I myself, choose only
to flee the horrors.

To ascribe evil to traumatic birth circumstances,
or karmic retribution, doesn't feel to be the
core of origination...but, who is to say?

Who is to say?

Prophet By The Side Of The Road

An old man sat on the curb near the park
an ancient face, deeply creased, white hair, like tufts of grass,
forcing its way out of the grey and red wool pull over cap,
a white beard with no particular shape hiding half his face,
blue eyes, Jesus eyes, looking out unblinkingly at the world
that walked past him....in it, but not of it.

His body was tightly folded like an accordion,
only the tan hands and dirty bare feet showed.
He was in dialogue with himself and an unseen other.

I thought of how the American Indians regarded these homeless
wanderers
as Holy and cared for them, bringing them food and clothing
and I wonder if we aren't really presumptuous today
thinking we know anything at all about the soul's intention,
when we call people, crazy.

Gratitude

I woke up this morning.
It was one of those beautiful soft autumn mornings
where you can hear the trees rustling and the pat
of runner's feet passing the house.
My bed was warm with its light flannel sheets
and my husband lay next to me, safe and
still sleeping.

48,000 people died in Pakistan 3 days ago in a moment.
Mudslides injured over 200,000 persons in Guatemala,
Louisiana, Florida and Texas, their cities flooded
discover more dead daily.
The wars go on in Afghanistan and Iraq.
Sons and young fathers die or are mutilated.
Africa's breasts have dried up and her children,
are starving. Aids is killing the world's
poorest women and children.

Sometimes I feel guilty my life is so comfortable,
my family safe and well fed.

Sometimes I feel I must pray more, serve more,
help more...hold a center of peace.

And on some mornings, mornings such as this one,
I think I need to just drop into the center of myself
and say "Thank you" to those souls making such sacrifices
to transform the consciousness of our planet.

Dear God, make it all worth it. Please.

The Black Queen

Psyche visited last night.
She said the Black Queen would have her due.

This is not the loving mother or compassionate friend.
This is the unforgiving warrior who takes no prisoners,
who remembers transgressions and omissions.

Like Iago she can whisper poisonous secrets in the ear of the King
or drop the golden apple of discord in a feminine gathering.
Her anger is not hot but icy.
Her tongue a lethal weapon.

I am placing a black orchid on her stone altar this morning.
A gift to this dark face of the moon.

Pan

He was a man that women were drawn to
like metal shavings to a magnet,
erudite, charming, vulnerable yet,
... clearly, carnivorous.

Animus women were particularly called.
He fed their need for fire, safely,
often from a distance.

Sometimes, they stood too close to the fire.

His wife said he was easier to love than to live with.

Sleep Walking

Her's seemed a small world
whose boundaries seldom expanded
beyond the mirror she
carried in her purse.

The listener was reduced to a pair of ears
and what was required, was just an occasional
nod of the head, indicating you had not
fallen asleep.

I wondered if one day, like the fabled princess
she would awaken, pop up and recognize, how many
people lived in the mirror along side of her,
how many lived in back and beyond it.

Would that be a marvelous gifting
or a mere disappointment?

Goldfish Philosophy

I knelt down to join the small boy who
had seated himself opposite the fish tank
in the waiting room of the dentist,
his hands under his chin,
his gaze intense and quiet.

Together we watched in silence
as the small colored fish swam
in and out of the sea plants.

He asked me if fish thought about things
and I said only a fish could say for sure,
but I believed they did.

He smiled and said, "I do too".

Denial

She knew the truth of the situation.
The conundrum lay in not wanting the truth
to be
what it was.

Becoming

Today I feel happy with who I have become
and more accepting of the process of becoming.
So often, I have felt my direction was not of
my own choosing, imposed on me by circumstance,
more crisis management than self actualization.
Now I know the person I've become
required this life

It Is Never Too Late

If all of life was reduced to
a single moment
when
we fully experienced
the miracle
of knowing beyond doubt
that we were a being of light,
timeless and eternal,
that all other beings,
were of light,
timeless and eternal,
we would have lived
a life
worthy
of life.

It is never too late.